The Best Advice Powered By Artificial Intelligence

PROFESSOR MARCO'S

TOP **20** TIPS

ON

GOLF

I0519036

FROM *NEW YORK TIMES* BESTSELLING AUTHOR

MARC OSTROFSKY

For general information on our products and services or to purchase bulk copies of this book, please contact us at books@marceting.com.

ISBN: 978-1-962979-00-9

Table of Contents

Introduction

Artificial Intelligence or A.I. is all the rage! We thought it would be fun to create a series of comprehensive yet easy-to-read books that compile all the best advice A.I has to offer. Our A.I.-powered project summarizes the top actionable tips explained by our also A.I.-generated character, Professor MarcO.

This book focuses on Golf.

What golfer doesn't want (or need) to improve their game? We've made this simple—with quick, easy-to-grasp tips on how to drive, pitch, chip, putt, and even hit out of the sand.

We have chosen the top 20 categories to improve your golf game, making an easy and concise list to quickly find all the answers in one place! From basics such as golf etiquette and rules you should always keep in mind on the course. to tips on improving your swing or choosing the correct club—it's all right here at your fingertips. Whether you are new to golf or an experienced golfer, this book is an excellent resource to keep in your golf bag and will help you become a better golfer.

So, let's begin!

Note from the Professor:

Golfers know that this sport is a lifelong pursuit of perfection. Yet in golf, as in life, perfection is not impossible, but it is always fleeting. Ask any low handicapper or professional golfer! Golf is about doing your best, one shot at a time. It's not about being perfect and always hitting great shots, but hitting "better bad shots."

Progress in golf requires ongoing dedication to consistent practice and skill development. Focus on specific aspects of the game, such as swing mechanics, short game skills, course management, mental resilience and physical fitness. Incorporating drills, seeking feedback from a qualified instructor, playing with experienced golfers, and regularly playing on the course are important components of improving your golf game.

It's essential—for your progress and your sanity—to enjoy the journey and continually strive to improve, rather than fixating on the idea of achieving perfection.

WHAT DOES IT TAKE TO BECOME A GREAT GOLFER?

Have you just started thinking about taking up golf? Or maybe you've been playing for a while already. Regardless of where you are in your golf journey, there are a few things you'll have to commit to in order to upgrade your performance.

Here are Professor MarcO's Top 20 Tips on what it takes to become a great golfer:

1. **Skill Development**: Mastering the fundamentals of golf, including grip, stance, and swing technique, is essential. Continual improvement and refinement of these skills are crucial as these are the foundation upon which all other golf skills are built.

2. **Consistent Practice**: Consistency is key in golf. Structured and purposeful practice sessions are necessary to develop and maintain skills. Dedicate time to practice different aspects of the game, such as driving, iron play, short game, and putting.

3. **Continuous Learning**: Great golfers have a thirst for knowledge and are constantly seeking to learn. Engaging a good coach can provide valuable insights and corrections that you may not be able to identify on your own.

4. **Experience and Play**: Playing regularly on different courses, in various conditions, and in competitive environments helps build experience, adaptability, and composure under pressure.

5. **Proper Equipment**: Ensure your clubs are properly fitted for your swing and playing style. Having well-fitted and suitable golf equipment, including clubs, balls, and other accessories, can enhance performance and consistency.

6. **Physical Fitness**: Regular exercise improves strength, flexibility, and endurance which can lead to more powerful and accurate shots and help prevent injuries.

7. **Mental Resilience**: Golf is mentally demanding. It requires the ability to stay focused, manage stress, maintain a positive mindset, and recover quickly after a bad shot or round.

8. **Emotional Control**: Managing emotions and staying composed, even in challenging situations, is crucial to making sound decisions and executing shots effectively.

9. **Patience and Persistence**: Progress in golf often comes in small increments. Great golfers understand the importance of patience, perseverance, and a long-term approach to improvement.

10. **Strategic Understanding**: It's not just about hitting the ball well; it's also about understanding the strategic aspects of the game to make smart decisions. Knowing when to take risks, understanding how different weather conditions affect play, and being able to plan ahead can all contribute to a lower score.

11. **Course Management**: Understanding how to strategize your game according to the layout and challenges of a specific golf course is crucial to improving your game.

12. **Adaptability**: Golf requires you to adjust and adapt to different types of courses, weather, and playing partners. Improving your ability to adapt to various conditions will make you a better golfer.

13. **Goal Setting**: Setting specific, measurable, and realistic goals helps maintain focus and motivation, providing a clear direction for improvement.

14. **Technology and Analytics**: Use modern technology to gather valuable data about your swing, ball flight, and other aspects of your game. Analyzing and understanding data and performance trends can provide valuable insights into areas for improvement and inform practice and strategy.

15. **Self-Assessment**: Regularly evaluating strengths and weaknesses, identifying areas for improvement, and working on specific aspects of the game can lead to significant progress.

16. **Competitive Spirit**: Developing a competitive mindset, both in practice and during play, fuels the drive to excel and constantly push boundaries.

17. **Smart Time Management**: Effectively managing time and balancing practice, play, physical fitness, and other commitments is essential for consistent improvement.

18. **Support System**: Having a supportive network, including coaches, mentors, training partners, and family, can provide guidance, encouragement, and accountability.

19. **Sportsmanship and Respect**: Great golfers embody sportsmanship and respect for the game, fellow competitors, and the golf course. They adhere to golf etiquette, demonstrate integrity, and appreciate the values and traditions of the sport.

20. **Love for the Game**: If you're not having fun, what is the point? Great golfers have a genuine passion and love for the game, which fuels their dedication, enjoyment, and long-term commitment.

Golf can be a challenging and sometimes frustrating sport, but golfers who achieve greatness are those who stick with it and continually work to improve to reach their full potential. Becoming a great golfer is a journey that requires patience, hard work, and a growth mindset. It's important to enjoy the process, embrace challenges, and continually strive for improvement while embracing the inherent beauty of the game.

"IF SUCESS IS BUILT ON FAILURE, I'M GOING TO BE *REALLY* SUCESSFUL ON THE GOLF COURSE SOMEDAY!"

TIPS FOR NEW GOLFERS

Whether you're taking your first swing or looking to refine your skills, these tips will serve as a compass on your golfing journey. This practical advice is a great reminder to bring it back to the basics.

Approaching golf with the right mindset, dedication, and a love for the sport will help you derive maximum enjoyment — and improvement — from your golf game.

Here are Professor MarcO's Top 20 Tips for new golfers:

1. **Start with proper instruction**: Take lessons from a qualified golf instructor to establish a strong foundation and avoid developing bad habits. A good instructor can help you identify and correct the flaws in your swing.

2. **Focus on fundamentals**: Master the basics first, emphasizing solid grip, posture, and alignment as the building blocks of a consistent swing.

3. **Practice regularly and with purpose**: Like any skill, regular and consistent practice is key. Be intentional in your practice sessions, focusing on specific areas for improvement rather than mindlessly hitting balls.

4. **Be patient**: Improvement in golf often comes slowly, so be patient with yourself and celebrate small victories along the way. Don't get discouraged if you don't see results immediately.

5. **Manage your expectations**: Golf is a challenging game that takes time to master. Accept that not every shot or round will be perfect. Focus on your own progress rather than comparing yourself to others.

6. **Stay positive**: Maintain a positive mindset, even when facing setbacks or difficult shots. Face each challenge or mistake as an opportunity to learn. Golf can be frustrating, but don't let a bad hole affect the rest of your game.

7. **Play within your abilities**: Don't try to hit shots that are beyond your skill level. Be aware of your limitations and make smart decisions on the course to avoid unnecessary risks.

8. **Keep a clear mind**: Trust your training and focus on the target. Avoid overthinking and cluttering your mind with too many swing thoughts.

9. **Learn to manage pressure**: Develop strategies for handling pressure situations, such as deep breathing, visualization, or positive self-talk.

10. **Get professionally fitted equipment**: Use equipment that suits your golf skill level and style of play. As you improve, your equipment needs might change. Start with clubs that fit your height, strength, and swing style. This can help you perform better and prevent injury.

11. **Play in different conditions**: Play in different weather conditions and on different types of courses to adapt your game.

12. **Develop a pre-shot routine**: Establishing a pre-shot routine helps you get in the right frame of mind for each shot, leading to more consistent performance.

13. **Focus on short game**: Before focusing on your drive, dedicate ample time to chipping, pitching, and putting. Learn to read the greens, as your short game can make or break your game.

14. **Visualize your shots**: Before swinging, visualize the shot you want to make. This helps with focus and can improve your execution.

15. **Mind your etiquette**: Be respectful of the course and other golfers. Learn and respect the rules and unwritten etiquette of golf, including not talking during someone else's swing and repairing the course after your shots.

16. **Invest in good golf shoes**: Comfort and stability are crucial in golf. As simple as it sounds, a good pair of golf shoes can improve your balance and prevent slipping during your swing.

17. **Learn from others**: Challenge yourself by playing with golfers of varying skill levels to learn from their strategies and techniques. Study professional golfers and analyze their techniques to gain insights and inspiration.

18. **Stay physically fit**: Golf requires physical strength, especially in your core and shoulders, as well as flex-ibility. Regular exercise can help improve your game and prevent injuries.

19. **Stay hydrated and energized**: Golf rounds can be long. Make sure to drink plenty of water and have healthy snacks on hand to maintain your concentration and stamina.

20. **Have fun**: Remember that golf is a game, and the primary objective is to have fun! Get some exercise, enjoy the outdoors, and don't take it too seriously.

GOLF ETIQUETTE

Consider golf etiquette as the inherent social contract of the sport. By following these established standards, we show respect for our fellow golfers and keep the game flowing smoothly. It's about prioritizing safety, taking care of the course, embodying good sportsmanship, and ultimately making sure all golfers have an enjoyable experience while playing.

Here are Professor MarcO's Top 20 Tips for golf etiquette that every golfer should know and follow:

1. **Avoid distractions**: Show respect to fellow golfers by maintaining silence and avoiding unnecessary noise or movement that may distract other players. When a fellow golfer is preparing to swing or putt, be quiet. No talking, no noise. Their concentration is key.

2. **Be punctual**: Arrive on time for your tee time and adhere to the pace of play guidelines.

3. **Repair divots and ball marks**: Replace or repair divots on the fairway to maintain the course's condition, and repair ball marks on the green to keep them smooth and playable for others.

4. **Rake bunkers**: After hitting from a bunker, rake the sand to erase footprints and ensure fair playing conditions for others.

5. **Be mindful of pace of play**: Play at a reasonable pace to maintain the flow of the game and be considerate of other groups on the course.

6. **Yield to faster players**: If you are playing slower than the group behind you, be courteous and allow them to play through.

7. **Be ready to play**: Be ready when it is your turn to avoid unnecessary delays. Prepare for your shots by having the appropriate club ready, studying the yardage, and lining up your shot while others are playing.

8. **Limit practice swings**: Keep practice swings to a reasonable number and avoid unnecessary delays.

9. **Look before swinging**: Be aware of your position on the course and maintain a safe distance from other players. Never hit your shot until the group in front of you is out of range.

10. **Shout "Fore!"**: Okay, sometimes you just misjudge the distance or completely mis-hit your shot. Be mindful of your golf ball's trajectory and shout "fore" if it poses a potential danger to other players.

11. **Be mindful of others' lines**: Do not walk across or stand on another player's putting lines on the green (the imaginary line that connects the ball to the hole).

12. **Be aware of your shadow**: Avoid casting a shadow over another player's ball, their putting line, or the hole, when they are about to hit or putt.

13. **Replace flagstick carefully**: When removing or replacing the flagstick, do so gently to avoid damaging the hole, the greens, or the flagstick itself.

14. **Follow cart rules**: Adhere to cart rules and guidelines, such as staying on designated paths, and keeping carts off tee boxes and away from the greens to preserve the turf.

15. Silence cell phones: Turn off or silence your cell phone to avoid disruptions during play.

16. Be polite and courteous: Treat other golfers and course staff with respect by being courteous, considerate, and mindful of their presence on the course.

17. Be honest with your score: Maintain the integrity of the game by accurately counting and recording your scores.

18. Dress appropriately: Many courses have a dress code, so be sure to check before you arrive. Adhere to the dress code and ensure appropriate attire on the course.

19. Be responsible for your trash: Dispose of any trash or litter properly by using designated bins on the course.

20. Follow course rules and regulations: Familiarize yourself with the specific rules and regulations of the golf course you are playing and adhere to them.

Some of these guidelines are well established, some are common sense, and some are unwritten rules. By following these golf etiquette guidelines, you contribute to a positive and respectful golfing experience for yourself and others on the course.

GOLF RULES

Understanding and following the rules of golf is essential for fair and enjoyable play.

Here are Professor MarcO's Top 20 Tips on golf rules:

1. **Teeing Off**: You must start each hole by teeing off behind the designated tee markers.

2. **Order of Play**: The player with the lowest score on the previous hole has the "honors" and tees off first on the next hole. Thereafter, the player furthest from the hole plays first, including on the green.

3. **Out of Bounds**: If your ball goes out of bounds, add one penalty stroke and replay from the spot of your previous shot.

4. **Lost Ball**: If you can't find your ball within three minutes, it is considered lost. Add one penalty stroke and play another ball from the same spot of the previous shot.

5. **Provisional Ball**: If you think your ball may be lost (not in a penalty area) or out of bounds, you can play a provisional ball to save time. However you must declare it as a provisional ball before playing it.

6. **Play the Ball as it Lies**: Unless a rule allows it, the ball must be played as it lies.

7. **Unplayable Lies**: If you deem your ball unplayable, you can take a one-stroke penalty and drop your ball within two club lengths of the original spot, no nearer the hole.

8. **Water Hazards**: If your ball lands in a water hazard (yellow penalty area), for a one-stroke penalty, you have the option of taking "stroke-and-distance relief"

by playing from where the original stroke was made, or taking "back-on-the-line relief" by dropping the ball on a reference line going straight back from the hole through the point where the original shot crossed the penalty area.

9. **Lateral Water Hazards**: If your ball goes into a lateral water hazard (red penalty area), you will incur a one-stroke penalty and have the same relief options as above. You also have a third option, and may drop within two club lengths of the point where your ball last crossed into the penalty area, not closer to the hole.

10. **Immovable Obstructions**: If your ball is obstructed by an artificial object, such as a cart path or a sprinkler head, you may take relief without penalty. The same goes for abnormal course conditions, such as an area of casual water or an area marked as ground under repair.

11. **Movable Obstructions**: You can remove loose impediments (natural objects like leaves and twigs) except when your ball and the loose impediment lie in the same hazard, such as a bunker.

12. **Grounding**: In a bunker, you are not allowed to touch the sand with your club prior to your downswing. Your club can only touch the sand when striking the ball.

13. **On the Putting Green**: On the putting green, you can mark, lift, clean, and replace your ball, and are allowed to repair ball marks and old hole plugs. You must replace your ball in the same spot.

14. **Flagstick**: If you are putting, you have the option to leave the flagstick in the hole or have it removed. There is no penalty for hitting the flagstick while putting from the green.

15. Ball at Rest Moved: If your ball is accidentally moved by you or your equipment, you generally incur a one-stroke penalty and must replace the ball. On the putting green, you may replace the ball without penalty.

16. Ball Interfered with by Another Player: If your ball is accidentally moved by another player, there is generally no penalty, and the ball is replaced.

17. Keeping Score: Keep track of your score for each hole and ensure accuracy when submitting your final score. Sign your scorecard once the round is complete.

18. Practice Swing: If you accidentally hit your ball during a practice swing on the tee, the ball is not considered in play and no penalty stroke is incurred. However once the ball is in play, the stroke counts and the ball is played from where it comes to rest.

19. Mulligans: In official play, mulligans (re-doing a shot without penalty) are not allowed. They are usually reserved for casual or charity events.

20. Etiquette: Respect for the course and other players is expected. Respect the etiquette and spirit of the game, including being honest, courteous, and considerate of other players on the course.

These are just a few of the many rules in golf that will provide a foundation for your golfing journey, ensuring fairness, safety, and sportsmanship on the course. It's important to familiarize yourself with the complete rules of golf, as published by the governing bodies, such as the United States Golf Association (USGA). This is a good list to get you started, especially for a casual golfer! You will learn more along the way.

THE PHYSICAL
ASPECTS OF GOLF

Note from the Professor:

> We all need to ask the right question to get the right answer. I asked A.I. a question about the physical aspects of golf and got the right answer to what was the wrong question.
>
> When I asked for "physical issues" in golf, I got back some of the physical **problems** and **injuries** that golfers deal with—which made me laugh! But, it's pretty accurate, so I included this list in the book as a bonus section!
>
> Don't let this scare you, though—we'll follow it up with the top tips to prevent these issues. For better or worse, here you go!

Here are Professor MarcO's Top 20 physical issues that golfers often encounter:

1. **Golfer's elbow** (Medial Epicondylitis): Overuse of the muscles in the forearm from the repetitive motion of the wrist and arm can result in pain and inflammation on the inside of the elbow.

2. **Tendinitis in the wrist**: Overuse and stress from the golf swing can lead to inflammation and pain in the tendons of the wrist.

3. **Carpal Tunnel Syndrome**: Repetitive gripping and swinging can put pressure on the nerve in the wrist, leading to numbness, tingling, and pain.

4. **Hand and finger injuries**: Gripping the club tightly or repetitive impact can lead to hand and finger pain or injuries, particularly with poor technique or grip.

5. **Trigger Finger**: This occurs when a finger or thumb gets stuck in a bent position due to inflamed tendons.

6. **Tennis elbow (Lateral Epicondylitis)**: Overuse of the muscles on the outside of the elbow can result in pain and inflammation.

7. **Shoulder injuries**: The golf swing places stress on the shoulders, leading to potential injuries or discomfort.

8. **Rotator cuff injuries**: The rotational forces involved in the golf swing can lead to rotator cuff strains or tears.

9. **Back pain**: Rotational swing mechanics and repetitive motion can contribute to back strain and discomfort.

10. **Neck pain**: Poor swing mechanics and posture can lead to neck pain and stiffness.

11. **Herniated disc**: The twisting and turning motions of the golf swing can cause pain, numbness, or weakness in the spine.

12. **Hip pain**: The hip joint can be strained or injured due to its rotational movement and weight-bearing role in the golf swing.

13. **Knee pain**: Twisting and pivoting motions during the swing can put stress on the knees, leading to pain or injury.

14. **Shin splints**: These can occur from excessive walking, especially on hilly courses.

15. **Plantar fasciitis**: The repetitive weight transfer and walking involved in golf can contribute to inflammation of the plantar fascia in the foot.

16. **Foot and ankle injuries**: Golfers may experience ankle sprains or strains due to uneven terrain or incorrect foot placement during the swing.

17. **Muscle imbalances**: Golfers may develop muscle imbalances, such as tightness in some areas and weakness in others, due to the one-sided nature of the swing.

18. **Dehydration**: Inadequate hydration can lead to fatigue, decreased focus, and potential performance decline.

19. **Lack of flexibility**: Limited flexibility can affect the golf swing, reducing range of motion and potentially leading to injuries.

20. **Lack of cardiovascular endurance**: Fatigue during a round can impact performance and consistency.

Insufficient overall fitness, including strength, flexibility, and balance, can hinder performance and increase the risk of injuries. With golf, repeating the same motions repeatedly can lead to overuse injuries in various areas of the body.

PHYSICAL FITNESS & TRAINING

It's important to minimize the risk of these physical issues and injuries by incorporating exercises, stretching, proper warm-ups, and maintaining overall fitness.

> *Before starting a new exercise regimen, consider consulting with a fitness professional or physical therapist to ensure that you're doing the exercises correctly and that they're appropriate for your level of fitness and any pre-existing conditions. If you are experiencing any persistent pain or discomfort, it's important to seek professional medical advice.*

Here are Professor MarcO's Top 20 Tips on physical fitness & training exercises to become a better golfer:

1. **Warm-up routine**: Perform dynamic warm-up exercises to prepare the body for the physical demands of golf and help prevent injuries.

2. **Stretching and flexibility**: Incorporate a stretching routine targeting all major muscle groups to maintain flexibility. Practicing Yoga and Pilates can help improve balance, flexibility, and range of motion.

3. **Balance training**: Single-leg exercises, stability ball, and balance board exercises can improve your stability for a more effective golf swing.

4. **Core strength**: Core strengthening exercises like planks, crunches, Russian twists, and bridges enhance stability and power generation, which will improve your swing mechanics.

5. **Rotational exercises**: Exercises like cable woodchops or medicine ball rotational throws improve your torso's range of motion and power for a better golf swing.

6. **Strength training**: Lifting weights and compound exercises such as squats, deadlifts, and lunges to build overall strength and power, enabling you to hit the ball harder and more accurately.

7. **Leg and glute strength**: Squats, lunges, leg presses, step-ups, and calf raises develop the strength and power you need to generate clubhead speed during your swing.

8. **Wrist and forearm strength**: Exercises like wrist curls and dumbbell wrist flexion and extension improve your grip and control of the club.

9. **Hand and grip strength**: Squeezing stress balls, using grip strengtheners, and performing finger stretches can improve hand strength and grip control.

10. **Resistance band exercises**: Utilize resistance bands to target muscles involved in the golf swing, such as shoulder external and internal rotations for the rotator cuff or trunk rotations.

11. **Shoulder mobility**: Arm circles, shoulder rolls, and chest openers help increase the range of motion in your shoulders, arms, and back.

12. **Neck and cervical spine exercises**: Neck stretches and strengthening exercises promote stability and reduce tension.

13. **Hip mobility**: Hip stretches and exercises like hip circles, lunges, and squats will improve hip rotation and flexibility during the swing.

14. **Hamstring stretches**: Tight hamstrings can limit your hip mobility and impact your golf swing. Try hamstring stretches like the seated or standing hamstring stretch.

15. **Ankle mobility**: Ankle circles, toe curls, and calf stretches improve ankle mobility and stability.

16. **Posture exercises**: Exercises that target the upper back and shoulders, such as rows and shoulder retractions, promote better posture throughout the swing.

17. **Cardio and endurance training**: Activities like jogging, cycling, swimming, or using an elliptical machine can increase your overall stamina, so you don't tire easily on the course.

18. **Interval training**: Mix in high-intensity interval training (HIIT) workouts to improve cardiovascular fitness and simulate the demands of the golf course.

19. **Plyometric exercises**: Jumping exercises like box jumps or medicine ball slams improve power and explosiveness.

20. **Rest and recovery**: Remember to take rest days and use techniques like foam rolling or gentle yoga to help your muscles recover.

Remember to consult with a fitness professional or golf-specific trainer to ensure proper form and technique when performing these exercises. A well-rounded physical training routine will contribute to improved performance, injury prevention, and overall enjoyment of the game.

THE MENTAL GAME OF GOLF

Golf is as much a mental game as it is a physical one. The mind plays a significant role in how well you perform on the course. So, it is paramount for golfers to consider and work on the mental aspects of golf alongside their physical skills.

Here are Professor MarcO's Top 20 Tips to improve your mental game when playing golf:

1. **Focus**: Maintain concentration on each shot and block out distractions.

2. **Confidence**: Believe in your ability and trust your swing.

3. **Positive attitude**: Adopt a positive mindset and approach challenges with optimism.

4. **Patience**: Golf is a game of waiting – for other players, for the wind, for the perfect shot. Practicing patience will serve you well.

5. **Resilience**: Learn to move on and bounce back from bad shots, bad holes, and bad rounds. The ability to let go of mistakes and focus on the next shot is key.

6. **Visualization**: Visualize successful shots and imagine the desired outcome before executing.

7. **Routine**: Establish a pre-shot routine to create consistency and prepare mentally for each shot.

8. **Mental stamina**: Stay mentally strong and resilient, even under pressure or in challenging situations.

9. **Emotional control**: Manage emotions, avoiding anger or frustration that can negatively impact performance.

10. **Adaptability**: Adapt to varying weather conditions, courses, and your own performance on a given day.

11. **Focus on the process**: Concentrate on executing each shot to the best of your abilities rather than worrying about the result.

12. **Acceptance**: Embrace the unpredictability of golf and accept that not every shot will be perfect.

13. **Mindfulness**: Stay present and in the moment, avoiding distractions or past mistakes and focusing on the task at hand.

14. **Goal setting**: Set realistic and achievable goals for each round or practice session to keep you motivated.

15. **Strategic thinking**: Golf is a strategic game. Think multiple shots ahead and make smart decisions based on your strengths and the course layout.

16. **Pressure management**: Develop strategies to perform well under pressure, such as deep breathing or positive self-talk.

17. **Discipline**: Stick to your game plan, even when things aren't going well. Persist and keep trying.

18. **Learning mentality**: Be open to learning from each round, each shot, and each mistake. Use every opportunity to improve.

19. **Respect**: Show respect for the course, the rules, and your fellow players. Don't allow anger or frustration to cloud your judgment.

20. **Gratitude**: Appreciate the opportunity to play a game you enjoy. Remember to maintain a sense of fun and enjoyment, keeping golf in perspective as a recreational activity.

Your mental approach to golf will directly influence your performance, your enjoyment of the game, and ultimately, your success as a golfer. Being able to bounce back from a poor shot, a bad hole, or even a disappointing round is a mark of a great golfer. This requires mental toughness and a short memory for mistakes. Always remember it is a game that is meant to be fun! It's a continuous process, so focus on developing these mental skills over time.

GOLF EQUIPMENT

The right golf equipment can significantly impact your performance on the course. Well-suited golf clubs, specifically tailored to your swing speed and style, can optimize your power, accuracy, and control. However, equipment can be an investment, so it's important to consider a variety of factors.

Here are Professor MarcO's Top 20 Tips for getting the right equipment in golf:

1. **Get fitted for clubs:** This is the most important thing you can do to ensure that you have the right equipment. A good fitter will take into account your height, weight, swing speed, and other factors to recommend the right clubs for you. Opt for a professional club fitting session to determine the appropriate specifications for your clubs, including shaft length, flex, and lie angle.

2. **Try before you buy**: Test different clubs and equipment to determine what feels comfortable and suits your playing style. You can attend demo days or golf expos where you can try out different equipment, or borrow from friends to test different brands and models before making a purchase.

3. **Consider your budget**: Determine your budget range and find equipment that offers the best value for your investment.

4. **Consider your skill level**: Choose equipment that matches your skill level and swing characteristics. Beginners may benefit from forgiving and game improvement clubs, while advanced players might prefer more specialized options.

5. **Assess your needs**: Identify the areas of your game that need improvement and select equipment that can address those specific needs.

6. **Understand club types**: Familiarize yourself with different club types, including drivers, woods, irons, wedges, and putters, and their specific purposes.

7. **Pay attention to clubhead design**: Different clubhead designs, such as cavity back or muscle back irons, can affect forgiveness, feel, and playability.

8. **Consider club fitting for wedges**: Fine-tuning your wedges through club fitting can help optimize loft, bounce, and grind options for improved short game performance.

9. **Understand shaft options**: The shaft is one of the most important parts of a golf club. Consider the material, flex, and weight of the shaft, as they can greatly impact the performance and feel of the club.

10. **Choose the right grip**: The grip affects the way you hold the club and the way the club feels in your hands. Choose a grip that is the right size for your hand, and explore different grip materials and textures for comfort and control.

11. **Consider adjustability**: Some clubs offer adjustable features, allowing you to fine-tune loft, lie, or weight distribution to optimize performance.

12. **Don't forget about the putter**: Putters are about feel and alignment – get one that inspires confidence. Spend time experimenting with different putter styles, shapes, and lengths to find one that suits your stroke and feels comfortable.

Note from the Professor:

> *Most golfers will agree that golf clubs, especially putters, seem to work great BEFORE they are purchased – and not as much AFTER they are purchased!*

13. **Research and read reviews**: Look for reputable sources and read reviews to gather information on equipment performance and quality. Do your research to ensure you're getting the best equipment for your needs and budget – don't be afraid to shop around for the best deals.

14. **Seek out reputable brands**: Invest in well-known, reputable, and respected golf equipment brands that have a track record of producing high-quality products.

15. **Avoid impulse buying**: Take your time to research, test, and compare equipment options before making a decision.

16. **Consider your playing conditions**: Think about the typical courses and conditions you play in and choose equipment suitable for those environments.

17. **Buy the right golf balls**: Experiment with different golf ball brands and models to find the right one for your game. The ball you choose will affect the way the ball flies and reacts on the greens. Make sure to choose a ball that is the right size, weight, and compression for your swing speed.

18. **Don't overlook the glove**: A proper golf glove can help improve your grip, particularly in hot or rainy weather.

Choose a glove that fits well and provides grip without compromising comfort.

19. **Research club technology**: Stay informed about the latest advancements in club technology and how they may benefit your game.

20. **Stay open to upgrades**: As your game improves, reassess your equipment needs and be open to upgrading clubs to match your evolving skills and preferences.

Getting the right golf equipment is a personal and individualized process. Take your time, seek expert advice, and choose equipment that feels comfortable and suits your game. Investing in suitable golf equipment, while also considering one's skill level and budget, is an essential step towards ensuring a positive golf experience.

Note from the Professor:

> *For beginners, the right technique is more beneficial than expensive equipment. Invest in lessons before splurging on top-tier clubs!*

IRONS & HYBRIDS

Here we will break down the different types of irons and hybrid clubs, when to use them, and how to hit them properly.

WEDGES

Wedges are considered a sub-set of irons due to their similar clubhead design, but they are the clubs with the highest loft—the largest angle between the clubface and the ground. This makes them launch the ball higher, making them ideal for shorter approach shots into greens, for chips and pitches around greens, and for playing out of sand bunkers.

1. **Pitching Wedge (PW)**: The pitching wedge is the most common wedge available and follows the 9-iron in loft, design, and feel. It is typically used for shorter approach shots and shots around the green. Position the ball in the center or slightly forward in your stance, make a controlled swing, and aim to strike the ball with a descending blow.

2. **Gap Wedge (GW)**: The gap wedge is used to bridge the gap in loft between the pitching wedge and sand wedge. It can be used for various shots around the green and shorter approach shots. Use a similar technique to the pitching wedge, adjusting the swing length and speed to control the distance.

3. **Sand Wedge (SW)**: The sand wedge is primarily used to get out of bunkers, but it can also be used for short chips and pitches around the green. With a high loft,

it produces a lot of height and spin. When hitting a sand wedge, open the clubface slightly, position the ball slightly forward in the stance, and aim to slide the clubhead under the ball to generate a high, soft shot.

4. **Lob Wedge (LW)**: The lob wedge has the highest loft among the wedges and is used for delicate shots around the green where height and precision are required. It is used for very short shots, particularly those that require high loft to stop quickly on the green. Open the clubface even more than with a sand wedge, position the ball forward, and make a controlled swing with a shallow angle of attack to produce a high, soft landing.

IRONS

Irons have angled faces etched with grooves that help grip the golf ball and impart spin. As the number of an iron goes up, the loft increases while the length of the shaft decreases. They are generally used on shots from the fairway, or for tee shots on short holes.

5. **9-Iron**: The 9-iron is a high lofted club used for moderate approach shots, typically within 130-140 yards. Position the ball slightly forward in the stance, make a controlled swing, and focus on a descending strike to create a piercing trajectory and control the distance.

6. **8-Iron**: The 8-iron is slightly less lofted than the 9-iron and can be used for longer approach shots within 140-150 yards or shots requiring more roll out. Use a similar technique to the 9-iron, adjusting the swing length and speed to control the distance.

7. **7-Iron**: The 7-iron is a versatile club used for approach shots from longer distances, typically within 150-165 yards. Position the ball slightly forward in the stance, make a smooth and controlled swing, and aim for a balanced strike to achieve a mid-trajectory shot.

8. **6-Iron**: The 6-iron is a shorter iron with a lower loft and is used for longer approach shots, around 165-180 yards. Position the ball slightly forward in the stance, make a sweeping swing, and focus on a clean strike to achieve a penetrating trajectory and maximize distance.

9. **5-Iron**: The 5-iron is a lower lofted club used for longer approach shots around 180-195 yards or shots requiring distance and control. Position the ball slightly forward in your stance, make a controlled and fluid swing, and focus on a solid strike to achieve a lower trajectory and increased distance.

10. **4-Iron**: The 4-iron is a challenging club to hit due to its low loft and longer length, used for long shots from 195-210 yards. It is typically used for long approach shots and tee shots on shorter, tighter holes. Use a similar technique to the 5-iron, but ensure a clean and solid strike to generate maximum distance.

11. **3-Iron**: The 3-iron is a mid-range iron, typically used for long shots where distance is the priority but you need more control than a wood can provide. Position the ball slightly forward, make a smooth and controlled swing, and focus on a solid strike to achieve a low trajectory and maximize distance.

12. **2-Iron**: The 2-iron is typically used for distance off the tee or from the fairway, especially when accuracy is most important. It is great for low shots under wind or on fast fairways. Due to its need for high swing speed and accurate strike, it's considered challenging to hit.

Many opt for easier-to-hit hybrids that can provide similar distances.

HYBRIDS

Some golfers replace their long irons (2-, 3-, 4- or 5-irons) with hybrid clubs, which have become increasingly popular in golf due to their combination of the ease of hitting of a fairway wood with the accuracy of an iron. The larger clubhead and lower center of gravity make them easier to hit and less prone to mis-hits.

Hybrids are versatile clubs that can be used in a variety of situations, including off the tee, fairway shots, and shots from the rough. They are designed to launch the ball higher and provide more distance compared to the equivalent iron. The combination of loft and clubhead design allows for optimal ball flight and distance performance. Hybrids are especially useful for shots from the rough or tight lies where long irons may struggle. The wider sole and lower center of gravity help the club glide through the turf and provide better contact and control.

13. **2-Hybrid**: The 2-hybrid, also known as a "rescue" club, is typically used as a replacement for a 5-wood or 2-iron. It has a slightly larger clubhead and a lower center of gravity, making it easier to launch the ball higher and achieve more distance compared to the equivalent iron. To hit it properly, place the ball in the middle of your stance and make a smooth, sweeping swing.

14. **3-Hybrid**: The 3-hybrid is a versatile club that replaces the 3-iron. It offers a combination of distance and control, making it useful for longer approach shots and tee shots on par-3 holes. The 3-hybrid is easier

to hit than the 3-iron due to its larger sweet spot and more forgiving design. To hit a 3-hybrid, position the ball slightly forward in your stance and maintain a steady rhythm in your swing.

15. **4-Hybrid**: The 4-hybrid is designed to replace the 4-iron and provide easier playability. It offers a higher launch and forgiveness compared to the equivalent iron, making it useful for longer approach shots and shots from the rough. The 4-hybrid is especially beneficial for golfers who struggle with consistent ball-striking using long irons.

16. **5-Hybrid**: The 5-hybrid is designed to replace the 5-iron and provide a higher launch and more forgiveness. It is ideal for longer approach shots, shots from the rough, or tee shots on par-3 holes. The 5-hybrid is easier to hit than the 5-iron, allowing golfers to achieve greater distance and control.

17. **6-Hybrid**: The 6-hybrid combines the forgiveness and playability of a hybrid club with the loft and distance characteristics of a 6-iron. It is particularly useful for longer approach shots, shots from the rough, or shots where a higher trajectory and more forgiveness are desired.

18. **7-Hybrid**: The 7-hybrid has a design more akin to a wood than an iron, which tends to make it more forgiving on mis-hits and easier to launch the ball high into the air. This can be particularly useful for shots that need to carry over hazards or need to land softly on the green. It is also often used from challenging lies in the rough or from fairway bunkers, where the wider sole can help slide through the turf or sand more easily than a 7-iron.

19. **8-Hybrid**: The 8-hybrid is designed to replace the 8-iron or even 9-iron for some players. The 8-hybrid really shines in challenging situations such as hitting from the rough or fairway bunkers. Its design makes it easier to get the ball airborne from these tricky positions compared to traditional irons. It's also a popular choice for those difficult shots where precision is more valuable than distance, like approach shots into tight greens or shots that need to navigate around obstacles.

20. **9-Hybrid**: The 9-hybrid provides a higher launch and increased forgiveness compared to a traditional 9-iron. It would be used for similar shots as a 9-iron but may provide more consistency, especially from challenging lies or rough terrain. The 9-hybrid is particularly useful for shorter approach shots, bunker shots, or shots from challenging lies that require precision and control, or other situations where a high, arcing shot is beneficial.

Remember, hybrids are designed to provide a more forgiving and playable alternative to long irons. They can be valuable additions to your golf bag, offering increased distance, versatility, and confidence when facing longer shots.

SWING PATH & ALIGNMENT

Swing path and alignment significantly impact the direction and consistency of your shots.

SWING PATH

The swing path refers to the direction in which the clubhead travels during the swing, specifically the path it takes as it approaches the ball at impact.

The swing path can be categorized as either inside-out, outside-in, or neutral:

- **Inside-out path**: When the clubhead approaches the ball from inside the target line, it promotes a right-to-left ball flight (for right-handed golfers), often known as a draw. This path is desirable for generating power and distance.

- **Outside-in path**: When the clubhead approaches the ball from outside the target line, it promotes a left-to-right ball flight (for right-handed golfers), commonly referred to as a fade or slice. This path can lead to a loss of distance, accuracy, and inconsistency.

- **Neutral path**: A neutral swing path occurs when the clubhead approaches the ball along the target line, resulting in a straight or slightly controlled curve in either direction.

The swing path plays a critical role in determining the initial direction and curve of the ball flight. By developing a consistent and appropriate swing path, you can enhance accuracy, control, and the ability to shape your shots according to your intentions.

Here are Professor MarcO's Top 10 Tips to help you fix your swing path:

1. **Understand the desired swing path**: Learn about the proper swing path for your desired shot shape (straight, draw, or fade) and understand how it differs from your current swing path.

2. **Start with a smooth takeaway**: Pay attention to the first few feet of your backswing. Aim to have a smooth and controlled takeaway, keeping the club on the correct path from the beginning.

3. **Engage your body for the backswing**: Rotate your body, not just your arms, during the backswing. Your shoulder turn should dictate the length of your backswing.

4. **Focus on lower body and hip rotation**: Initiate your downswing with your lower body to promote an inside-out swing path. Your hips and legs should start turning towards the target, followed by your torso, arms, and finally the club.

5. **Use alignment aids**: Utilize alignment sticks or visual aids to help you visualize and reinforce the correct swing path during practice.

6. **Practice with impact boards or strike plates**: Use impact boards or strike plates to get feedback on your club's interaction with the ground and ensure you're swinging on the correct path.

7. **Start with small swings**: Begin with chip or pitch shots to get a feel for the correct path, then gradually increase the length of your swing.

8. **Practice in slow motion**: Practice slow, deliberate swings to develop a feel for the correct swing path and to train your muscles to move along that path.

9. **Incorporate drills**: Practice specific drills that target swing path correction, such as the "gate drill" or "inside-out swing drill," to ingrain the proper path into your swing.

10. **Video analysis**: Record your swing and analyze it to identify any swing path issues. Compare it to the desired swing path or seek guidance from a professional for feedback.

Correcting your swing path takes time and practice. Be patient with yourself and focus on making gradual improvements. An extra tip that always applies—consider working with a qualified golf instructor who can assess your swing and provide tailored guidance.

Consistency and dedication to proper technique will help you develop a better swing path, leading to better ball striking and improved overall performance on the course.

ALIGNMENT

Alignment refers to the positioning of your body, clubface, and target line in relation to the target you want to hit, and is an essential part of perfecting your swing.

• **Body alignment**: Positioning your feet, hips, and shoulders parallel to the target line helps establish a proper alignment. Your body alignment should match the target or accommodate the desired shot shape (such as aiming slightly left for a fade or right for a draw).

• **Clubface alignment**: The clubface's alignment affects the direction of the ball flight. Aligning the clubface square to the target line at address is crucial for hitting straight shots.

- **Target line**: The target line represents the desired path the ball should take to reach the target. It serves as a reference for aligning your body and clubface.

Proper alignment helps you visualize and aim at the target, increasing the likelihood of hitting straight and accurate shots and leading to improved shot consistency and confidence.

Here are Professor MarcO's Top 10 Tips to help you fix bad alignment:

1. **Visualize a target line**: Imagine a straight line extending from the target through your ball and beyond. Align your body and clubface to this line.

2. **Align your feet, hips, and shoulders**: Position your feet, hips, and shoulders parallel to the target line. Check your alignment regularly during practice and play.

3. **Focus on clubface alignment**: Ensure that the clubface is square to the target line at impact. Pay attention to the clubface's alignment and make adjustments as needed.

4. **Align your eyes**: Position your eyes directly over the ball or slightly inside the target line. This helps you align the clubface accurately and improves your perception of the target.

5. **Check your body position**: Your knees should be slightly bent, and your upper body should lean over the ball from the hips with a straight back. Avoid excessive tilting or leaning that can lead to misalignment. Maintain a proper posture and balance throughout your swing.

6. **Use alignment targets**: Identify intermediate targets or points along the target line to help align your body and clubface accurately.

7. **Establish a routine**: Develop a consistent pre-shot routine that includes alignment checks. Take the time to ensure your alignment is correct before every shot.

8. **Use alignment tools**: Utilize alignment sticks or other visual aids to create reference points for proper alignment during practice sessions.

9. **Practice with mirrors**: Use mirrors during practice sessions to observe your setup, alignment, and swing. This visual feedback can help you make necessary adjustments.

10. **Video analysis**: Record your swing and analyze it to assess your alignment. Compare it to proper alignment models or seek feedback from a professional instructor.

Make sure you incorporate these tips into your practice routine consistently. Over time, with focused attention and repetition, you can improve your alignment and ensure that you're consistently aiming at your intended target. Seeking guidance from a qualified instructor can also be beneficial in correcting alignment issues and refining your technique.

DRIVING

A strong and accurate drive is critical in golf as it sets the tone for the rest of the hole. Spending time to practice and improve your driving skills is an essential part of improving your overall game.

Here are Professor MarcO's Top 20 Tips for improving your drive off the tee:

1. **Watch your tee height**: Experiment with tee heights to find the optimal level that allows you to strike the ball with the center of the clubface. A good rule of thumb is to have half the ball above the top of the driver when it's on the tee.

2. **Position the ball**: Place the ball just inside your front heel for ideal launch and contact.

3. **Master your grip**: Establish a firm, yet relaxed grip. A neutral grip helps keep the clubface square at impact and gives you better control over the club.

4. **Find the right stance**: Position your feet shoulder-width apart and align your body parallel to the target line.

5. **Maintain good posture**: Stand tall with a slight bend in your knees. Hinge forward from the hips with a straight back and relaxed arms.

6. **Control your backswing**: Initiate the backswing with a smooth and controlled movement of the clubhead, avoiding sudden jerks or excessive wrist movement.

7. **Focus on a relaxed and fluid swing**: Avoid tensing up and strive for a smooth, rhythmic swing that maximizes clubhead speed.

8. **Maintain a wide backswing arc**: Extend your arms fully and create a wide arc to maximize power and maintain control, increasing potential swing speed.

9. **Rotate shoulders**: Complete a full shoulder turn during the backswing to create torque and generate power.

10. **Create lag in the downswing**: Preserve the angle between the clubshaft and your lead arm until just before impact to generate power and clubhead speed.

11. **Lead with your hips**: Start your downswing by rotating your hips. Utilize the rotation of your hips and transfer of weight from back to front to generate power in your swing and keep the club on the correct path.

12. **Stay balanced**: Shift your weight smoothly from your back foot to your front foot during the downswing, maintaining during weight transfer. Keep your lower body stable during the swing to prevent swaying and inconsistent shots.

13. **Release the club through impact**: Allow the clubhead to release naturally through impact, avoiding excessive hand manipulation or flipping.

14. **Stay connected**: Keep your arms and torso connected through the swing for better control and consistency.

15. **Don't over swing**: Resist the urge to rush your swing or swing as hard as possible. A smoother, controlled swing often results in better contact and farther drives. Focus on a controlled and well-paced swing rather than swinging with maximum effort.

16. **Keep your on the ball**: Keep your eye on the ball from the start of the swing to solid contact. Avoid lifting your head prematurely, maintaining a steady head position to ensure good balance and more consistent contact.

17. **Square your clubface**: Aim to have your clubface square to your target at impact to ensure straight shots, minimizing the chance of hooks or slices.

18. **Follow through**: Finish the swing with a balanced and controlled follow-through, facing the target. This helps with power and direction.

19. **Play to your strengths**: Understand your tendencies and play a shot shape that suits your natural swing tendencies, whether it's a draw or a fade.

20. **Play strategically**: Evaluate the hole layout and select the appropriate club and shot shape to give yourself the best advantage. Prioritize accuracy over distance and aim for the center of the fairway to set up the next shot.

Remember, driving in golf is a skill that requires practice and refinement. Approach each drive with a positive mindset and believe in your abilities to execute a successful shot. Be patient, stay committed to improving, and enjoy the process of honing your driving abilities.

CHIPPING

Chipping in golf refers to a low-trajectory shot played from around the green, usually within about 30 yards. A chip shot is used when a golfer is near the green but needs to lift the ball over an obstacle, such as rough, fringe, or a bunker. The technique requires a controlled swing and precise contact with the ball, and aims to strike the ball with a lower trajectory so that it bounces and rolls on the green, mimicking the line of a putt. Golfers may use a wedge, short iron, or even a putter, depending on how much roll or loft the situation demands and the distance to the target.

Here are Professor MarcO's Top 20 Tips for chipping:

1. **Choose the right club**: Select a club with sufficient loft, such as a wedge or a short iron, based on the distance and trajectory you want to achieve.

2. **Establish a narrow stance**: Position your feet closer together than you would for a full swing to promote better balance and control.

3. **Position the ball back in your stance**: Place the ball slightly towards the back of your stance to ensure the ball is struck cleanly and at a descending angle.

4. **Maintain a light grip pressure**: Avoid gripping the club too tightly, as it can restrict your feel and touch around the greens. Keep your grip pressure light, your arms relaxed, and your swing smooth and unhurried.

5. **Choke down on the club**: Grip down a little on the club. This gives you more control and feel for the shot, which can improve accuracy.

6. **Keep your wrists firm**: Maintain firm wrists throughout the chipping motion. Your shoulders should control the chipping motion, not your wrists.

7. **Position hands ahead**: Make sure your hands are ahead of the ball at address. Your hands, or the grip end of the club, should be slightly closer to the target than the ball at setup. This promotes a downward strike on the ball, ensuring clean contact and the correct loft.

8. **Keep your weight forward**: Shift your weight slightly toward your front foot to encourage a downward strike and avoid thin or fat shots.

9. **Don't scoop**: Resist the urge to "lift" or "scoop" the ball into the air by flipping your wrist at impact. Instead, strike down and through the ball, letting the loft of the club do the work.

Note from the Professor:

> **What is a thin shot?** Also called "topping the ball," a thin shot occurs when the golfer strikes the ball with the bottom edge of the club, often hitting the middle of the golf ball rather than the bottom. This causes the ball to travel at a lower trajectory and goes further than intended.
>
> **What is a fat shot?** Also known as a "chunked shot," a fat shot occurs when the golfer's club hits the ground before making contact with the ball. This results in the club digging into the turf and the energy of the swing being absorbed by the ground instead of being transferred to the ball. Consequently, the ball doesn't travel as far as intended.

10. **Use a pendulum-like swing**: Maintain a smooth and consistent rhythm, creating a pendulum-like motion with your arms and shoulders to generate consistent contact and control.

11. **Maintain a shallow angle of attack**: Aim to strike the ball with a shallow, descending blow to promote a controlled, accurate chip shot.

12. **Control the length of your backswing**: A shorter backswing can give you more control over the distance of your chip shots. Practice varying the length of your backswing to develop a sense of distance control for different chip shots.

13. **Accelerate through the ball**: Always accelerate through the ball. Decelerating through impact can lead to poor contact and lack of distance control.

14. **Follow through**: Ensure your clubhead follows through towards the target. This helps to ensure the ball goes in the direction you intended.

15. **Read the green**: Assess the slope and grain of the green to anticipate how the ball will roll after landing, aiding in proper club selection and target placement.

16. **Aim for the landing spot**: Instead of looking at the hole, aim for a spot on the green where you want the ball to land before it rolls toward the hole. This target spot should take into account the slope and speed of the green.

17. **Practice, practice, practice**: Practice chipping from various lies, including uphill, downhill, and tight lies, to develop versatility and adaptability. Experiment with different club selections and swing lengths to develop the ability to chip the ball at varying heights and trajectories.

18. **Develop touch and feel**: Spend time practicing delicate, finesse chips to develop touch and feel around the greens, allowing for more precise distance control. Good chipping is often more about feel than technical perfection.

19. **Visualize the shot**: Take a moment to visualize the trajectory and landing spot of the chip shot, helping you execute the shot with more precision.

20. **Stay committed and confident**: Approach each chip shot with confidence, trust your technique, and commit to the shot you have chosen.

Consistent practice and experimentation are key to improving your chipping skills. A well-executed chip shot can put you on track for a birdie or even save par, while a sloppy chip can send your scorecard soaring. Mastering your chip shots sharpens your precision and control, and can boost your overall game.

PITCHING

In golf, pitching refers to a type of shot played from a relatively short distance, typically around the green, where the player needs to carry the ball over an obstacle or onto the putting surface with a controlled trajectory and spin, landing softly on the green with minimal roll.

The goal of pitching is to control the height, spin, and distance of the shot to accurately place the ball closer to the target. It is used when the player is too close to the green to make a full swing but too far to use a chip shot or a putt. Pitching involves a slightly longer backswing utilizing a wedge—such as a gap wedge, sand wedge, or lob wedge—with an accelerated downward strike, generating height and backspin to help the ball stop quickly upon landing.

Pitch shots require precision, touch, and the ability to vary the length of backswing and swing speed to control the distance and trajectory of the ball accurately.

Note from the Professor:

> You may be wondering, what is the difference between chipping and pitching?
>
> A **chip shot** is a low trajectory shot that spends more time rolling on the green than it does in the air. It's typically used when you're close to the green but not on it, and you want the ball to roll toward the hole like a putt after it lands on the green. Chipping usually involves a shorter backswing, a controlled downward strike, and minimal wrist movement to keep the ball low

and rolling upon landing. The club selection can vary from a 7-iron to a lob wedge, depending on how much roll or loft the situation demands.

*On the other hand, a **pitch shot** is a higher trajectory shot that spends more time in the air than it does rolling on the ground. It's typically used when you are a bit farther from the green and need to get the ball over an obstacle, such as a bunker or rough, or when the pin is placed near the edge of the green with little green to work with. Pitching typically involves a more lofted club like the sand wedge or a lob wedge. It requires a more substantial swing than chipping with a more aggressive strike to generate a higher trajectory and more backspin so the ball will stop more quickly once it lands.*

Here are Professor MarcO's Top 20 Tips for pitching:

1. **Use a lofted club**: Use a lofted club to get the ball high quickly and land softly. Select a wedge with appropriate loft, such as a gap wedge, sand wedge, or lob wedge, based on the distance and trajectory required for the pitch shot.

2. **Establish a narrow stance**: Position your feet closer together than you would for a full swing to promote better balance and control. Ensure your stance is square or slightly open to the target.

3. **Position the ball**: Place the ball in the center or slightly back in your stance to allow for clean contact and a descending strike.

4. **Maintain a relaxed grip**: Hold the club with a light grip pressure to enhance feel and touch and ensure a fluid swing. Grip down slightly lower on the club for better control.

5. **Keep your wrists firm**: Maintain firm wrists throughout the pitching motion. Avoid excessive wrist movement.

6. **Position hands ahead**: Your hands should be slightly ahead of the ball at address.

7. **Keep your weight forward**: Put most of your weight on the front foot throughout the swing for a better ball strike.

8. **Engage your body for control and power**: Utilize your body, particularly your shoulders and torso, to maintain a smooth and controlled pitching motion.

9. **Maintain a shallow angle of attack**: Aim to strike the ball with a shallow, descending blow to promote a controlled, accurate pitch shot.

10. **Hinge and hold**: Hinge your wrists on the backswing and hold through impact and follow-through.

11. **Control the length of your backswing**: Develop a smooth and consistent swing where the length of the backswing dictates distance, not a change in tempo or speed. Employ a backswing length that suits the distance and trajectory needed for the pitch shot.

12. **Generate power from your upper body rotation**: Initiate the downswing with a rotation of your upper body to generate power and maintain control.

13. **Utilize the bounce of the club**: Allow the bounce (curved bottom part) of the wedge to glide along the turf, preventing the leading edge from digging into the ground.

14. **Keep your eyes on the ball**: Keep your eyes on the ball through impact to ensure solid contact.

15. **Accelerate and follow through**: Accelerate through the shot, allowing your momentum to swing naturally through the ball after contact. Match the length of your backswing and follow-through.

16. **Consider the green conditions**: Assess the firmness or softness of the green to adjust your strategy and shot selection for optimal performance. Just like putting, consider any break on the green when targeting.

17. **Develop touch and feel**: Spend time practicing delicate, finesse pitch shots to develop touch and feel around the greens, allowing for more precise distance control.

18. **Visualize the shot**: Take a moment to visualize the trajectory and landing spot of the pitch shot, helping you execute the shot with more precision.

19. **Practice, practice, practice**: Practice pitch shots from various lies, including uphill, downhill, and tight lies, to develop versatility and adaptability. Spend time practicing pitch shots from different distances and varying the length of your backswing and the speed of your swing to develop a feel for distance control, trajectory, and accuracy.

20. **Play with confidence and commitment**: Approach each pitch shot with confidence, trust your technique, and commit to the shot you have chosen.

Consistent practice and experimentation are key to improving your pitching skills. Pay attention to the results of your pitch shots, evaluate your performance, and make necessary adjustments to improve consistency and accuracy. Focus on developing a solid foundation and technique while adapting to different situations on the course.

PUTTING

Putting requires patience and commitment to the process. Try to keep it simple—don't overthink your putts. Focus on the basics: line, speed, and contact. Embrace the challenge and remain dedicated to improving your putting skills over time.

Here are Professor MarcO's Top 20 Tips for improving your putting:

1. **Develop a consistent pre-shot routine**: Establish a pre-shot routine that includes a few practice strokes and a consistent setup routine to promote consistency and confidence.

2. **Establish your setup**: Find a consistent, comfortable stance that you can repeat, with your knees slightly bent and your feet shoulder-width apart. Position the ball just forward of the center of your stance.

3. **Use a light grip pressure**: Avoid gripping the putter too tightly. Hold the putter with a light and relaxed grip, allowing for a smooth stroke.

4. **Align your body and putter**: Ensure your body and putter are aligned parallel to the target line to promote accurate putts.

5. **Maintain a steady head**: Keep your head still until the ball is on its way. Moving your head during your putt can throw off your stroke.

6. **Keep your eyes directly over the ball**: Make sure your eyes are directly over the ball. Focus on a spot on the ball during the stroke, and do not lift your head until after you've hit the ball.

7. **Keep your wrists firm**: Avoid excessive wrist movement and maintain firm wrists to promote a consistent stroke. Use your shoulders to power the putt, keeping your arms and wrists still.

8. **Utilize a smooth, pendulum-like stroke**: Employ a pendulum-like motion with your arms and shoulders to create a smooth, rhythmic stroke. Ensure a smooth transition from the backswing to the forward stroke, avoiding any abrupt or jerky movements.

9. **Accelerate through the ball**: Maintain an accelerated stroke through impact to ensure solid contact and consistent roll.

10. **Follow through**: Don't abruptly stop your stroke after you hit the ball. Make sure your stroke continues smoothly after hitting the ball to help you hit the ball with more power and accuracy.

11. **Control the length of your backswing**: Develop a consistent backswing length—typically longer for greater distances, shorter for less. A controlled backswing is about consistency and developing a sense of feel and rhythm.

12. **Control the speed of your putts**: Focus on the speed and pace of your putts, considering the slope and distance to the hole. Practice different length putts to gain better speed control.

13. **Read the green**: Assess the slope, grain, and contours of the green to gauge the break and adjust your aim accordingly.

14. **Visualize the line and the roll**: Visualize the desired line and roll of the putt before addressing the ball, helping to align your stroke with your intended path.

15. **Aim small, miss small**: Aim for a smaller target within the hole to promote a more precise and focused stroke.

16. **Trust your line**: Once you've chosen your line, trust it. Doubt can cause you to make adjustments mid-stroke and miss the putt.

17. **Putt with confidence**: Approach each putt with confidence and a positive mindset, believing in your ability to make the putt.

18. **Get professionally fitted**: Ensure your putter is suited for your stroke. Experiment with different putters until you find one that feels comfortable and helps you to make more putts.

19. **Get a putting lesson**: Work with a qualified golf instructor to receive personalized guidance and feedback on your putting technique. They can provide personalized tips and corrections that you may not be able to identify yourself.

20. **Practice with a purpose**: Incorporate focused putting practice sessions, including drills and games, to hone your skills and develop a reliable putting stroke.

Because putting is so important to your overall game, here are a few extra tips for improving your putting:

21. **Practice short putts**: The ability to consistently sink short putts will significantly impact your score. Spend time practicing short putts to build confidence, eliminate unnecessary strokes, and avoid three-putts.

22. **Practice distance control**: Practice different length putts to develop a sense of distance control and feel for various speeds. Vary the length of your backswing and follow-through to hone your feel for how much backswing is required for different distances.

23. **Practice lag putting**: On longer putts, focus on distance control rather than getting the ball in the hole. Try to "lag" the ball as close to the hole as possible, setting up for an easier second putt and reducing the risk of three-putting.

24. **Prepare mentally**: Incorporate pressure situations into your practice to simulate on-course scenarios. Staying calm and focused, especially under pressure, can significantly improve your putting.

25. **Keep track of your statistics**: Track your putting statistics, such as putts per round and three-putt avoidance, to identify areas for improvement and monitor progress. Don't forget that each missed putt is an opportunity to learn.

Putting is a skill that requires practice and patience. Consistency and a calm approach are key to becoming a better putter. By incorporating these tips into your putting practice, seeking professional guidance when needed, and dedicating time to refine your technique, you can improve your putting skills and enhance your overall performance on the greens.

BUNKER & SAND SHOTS

Despite your best efforts, you'll inevitably end up in a bunker at some point. Practicing bunker shots will boost your confidence, help you manage the course better, and lower your scores.

Here are Professor MarcO's Top 20 Tips for hitting a bunker or sand shot:

1. **Select the right club**: Use a sand wedge or lob wedge that has enough loft to get the ball up and out. Consider using different clubs depending on the distance and trajectory required for the shot.

2. **Position the ball**: Place the ball slightly forward in your stance, typically off the inside of your left (or front) heel if you're right-handed, and vice versa if you're left-handed.

3. **Widen your stance**: Adopt a slightly wider stance to provide stability and maintain balance during the swing.

4. **Take an open stance**: Your feet, hips, and shoulders should be opened (aimed to the left for right-handed players) relative to the target line to encourage an out-to-in swing path.

5. **Dig your feet in**: Dig your feet into the sand for stability and to gauge the sand's depth and consistency.

6. **Open the clubface**: Open your clubface at setup to utilize the club's bounce, which helps to slide the club under the ball without digging into the sand.

7. **Soften grip**: Grip the club lightly to promote a relaxed and fluid swing, but firmly enough to prevent it from twisting in the sand.

8. **Keep your weight forward**: Shift your weight slightly onto your front foot to encourage a descending strike and prevent excess digging.

9. **Aim behind the ball**: Instead of focusing on the ball, visualize striking a spot about two inches behind the ball to allow the sand to lift the ball out of the bunker.

10. **Maintain a shallow angle of attack**: Aim to enter the sand just behind the ball with a shallow angle of attack, allowing the club to slide under the ball.

11. **Accelerate through impact**: Maintain an accelerating swing through the sand to ensure the clubhead strikes the sand before the ball and to generate the necessary power and loft.

12. **Swing along the body line**: Swing the club along your body line, allowing the club head to splash through the sand, swinging out towards the target.

13. **Control the backswing**: Keep the backswing smooth and controlled, avoiding excessive wrist action or lifting the club too steeply.

14. **Wrist hinge**: Maintain a slight wrist hinge in the backswing to generate power and club head speed.

15. **Trust the loft**: Use the loft of the club to get the ball out of the bunker. Avoid trying to lift the ball with excessive force.

16. **Maintain a steady head**: Keep your head steady throughout the swing to promote consistent contact.

17. **Finish with high hands**: Follow through with high hands and a full extension of the arms to ensure a complete and balanced finish.

18. **Maintain rhythm and tempo**: Focus on maintaining a smooth and consistent rhythm and tempo throughout the swing, avoiding rushed or decelerated motions.

19. **Practice different lies**: Practice bunker shots from various lies, including both plugged and fluffy lies, to develop versatility and adaptability. Consider the type of sand; you may need to swing harder for wet or compact sand than for loose sand.

20. **Practice with purpose**: Regularly dedicate time to bunker practice to develop a feel for the sand and improve your overall proficiency, focusing on technique, consistency, and distance control.

Mastering bunker shots takes practice and experience. Experiment with different techniques and find what works best for you. With time and dedication, you can develop the confidence and skill to navigate bunkers effectively and improve your overall game.

UPHILL & DOWNHILL LIES

It's hard enough to hit a good golf shot when the ball and your feet are on a flat lie. It's even harder when hitting a golf ball on an uphill or downhill sloping surface.

Here are Professor MarcO's Top 20 Tips to help you do just that.

THE UPHILL LIE

1. **Adjust your weight distribution**: Place more weight on your back foot, matching the incline of the hill, to maintain balance during the swing and help you swing up the slope.

2. **Align shoulders with slope**: Tilt your shoulders until they align parallel to the slope of the hill.

3. **Adjust ball position**: Position the ball slightly forward in your stance, closer to your higher foot, to encourage a more upward strike and a higher ball flight.

4. **Choose the right club**: Select a club with slightly less loft than you normally would for the given distance. The incline adds loft to the shot, causing the ball to fly higher and shorter.

5. **Play for extra distance**: Uphill shots also tend to lose distance, so consider this in your club selection to ensure you reach your target.

6. **Aim slightly right**: Aim slightly right of your target (for right-handed players). Your body won't rotate as much from an uphill lie as a level lie, so these shots tend to be pulled left. Account for this by adjusting your aim.

7. **Swing with the slope**: Allow your swing to follow the slope of the hill, which may result in a steeper swing plane.

8. **Maintain your posture**: Try to maintain your spine angle consistent with the slope throughout the swing, rather than keeping it vertical. This can aid in cleaner contact.

9. **Swing smoothly**: Focus on making a controlled and smooth swing to maintain balance and avoid excessive body movement.

10. **Shorten your backswing**: Consider shortening your backswing to help maintain balance. This will help you to keep the club on path and hit the ball with more accuracy.

THE DOWNHILL LIE

11. **Adjust your weight distribution**: Shift a bit more weight onto your front foot to help hit down and through the shot.

12. **Align shoulders, knees, and hips with slope**: Keeping your body parallel to the slope helps maintain balance and stability while keeping you from hitting behind or in front of the ball.

13. **Adjust ball position**: Position the ball slightly back in your stance nearer your higher foot to compensate for the slope and promote solid contact.

14. **Choose the right club**: The downhill slope will decrease the club's loft, making it travel farther with a lower trajectory. Account for this by selecting a more lofted club to make sure your ball launches higher.

15. **Anticipate distance**: The ball may travel further than usual due to the altered loft in a downhill lie. Consider this when selecting your club and target accordingly.

16. **Plan for extra roll**: Downhill shots will generally roll more upon landing, so plan your shot accordingly.

17. **Aim slightly left**: Aim slightly left of your target (for right-handed golfers). Downhill shots tend to go right because you're extending your arms down the slope, leaving the clubface open at impact. Aim a little left to compensate.

18. **Trace the slope**: Swing on the same plane as the hill to ensure smooth contact. Extend your arms through impact so that the clubhead travels as low to the slope as possible.

19. **Swing with controlled speed**: Use a controlled swing speed to maintain balance and prevent the club from digging into the ground. The downhill lie can disrupt balance, so avoid the temptation to swing too hard.

20. **Follow through**: Don't try to lift the ball into the air. Trust the loft of your club and let it do the work. Your follow-through may feel restricted due to the slope, which is normal in this scenario.

Practicing on various uphill and downhill lies is essential to develop a better understanding and feel for them.

Note from the Professor:

> *A rule of thumb for uphill and downhill lies: the ball should be closer to your higher foot and weight should favor your lower foot. However, there is conflicting advice on this—some golf pros teach the exact opposite! I suggest asking your instructor or experimenting with different adjustments to see what works best for you. What is most important is to remain balanced through the swing and make clean contact.*

AVOIDING SLICES & HOOKS

THE SLICE, THE FADE & THE PUSH

In golf, a slice, a fade, and a push are terms used to describe different types of ball flights with a rightward trajectory for right-handed golfers (or leftward for left-handed golfers). They are primarily determined by the clubface orientation and swing path at the moment of impact.

Here's a brief explanation of each:

Slice: A shot that curves severely from left to right for right-handed players (or vice versa for left-handed players). It is usually unintentional and due to an open clubface at impact combined with an outside-in swing path, causing a clockwise sidespin on the ball.

The ball travels relatively straight, then veers off to the right of the intended target (or left for left-handed golfers).

Fade: A shot where the golf ball curves gently from left to right for a right-handed player (or vice versa for a left-handed player). This typically results from a slightly outside-in swing path with the clubface slightly open relative to the path.

Unlike a slice, a fade is a deliberate shot shape that can be used strategically to maneuver around obstacles, play against the wind, or approach the green from an advantageous angle.

Push: A shot that travels relatively straight but ends up right of the target for right-handed players (or vice versa for left-handed players). It can be the result of bad alignment—hitting it straight but aimed to the right—or when the swing path is inside-out with the clubface square to that path, causing the ball to start right and continue in that direction.

There is no question that the slice is the #1 miss for the majority of amateur players. Here are Professor MarcO's Top 10 Tips to fix the dreaded slice:

1. **Control clubface angle**: Pay attention to your clubface at impact. If you're consistently hitting slices, it means your clubface is open at impact. The key is to identify why. To reduce your slice, you need to correct the clubface so it's more square at impact.

2. **Focus on swing path**: Utilize the swing path that matches your desired shot shape. A slice occurs from an over-the-top swing motion and an open clubface. Identify what factors are contributing to your outside-to-inside swing path and practice swinging straight through the line of the ball on your downswing.

3. **Check your grip**: Slices can be a result of a weak grip, where the hands are rotated more towards the left (for right-handed golfers). This tends to lead to taking the club too far inside, and can cause the clubface to open—hence your slice. Adjust your hand position for a more neutral grip.

4. **Relax your grip pressure**: Avoid gripping the club too tightly, as it can limit the wrist movement and fluidity of your swing, causing an open clubface. Maintain a relaxed grip pressure to promote a smoother release of the club.

5. **Monitor your alignment**: Make sure your body and clubface are aligned properly with the target. Practice setting up square to the target to promote more accurate shots.

6. **Adjust ball position**: If you're trying to hit a fade, the ball should be positioned more forward in your stance. However, if you keep slicing it, experiment with moving the ball slightly back in your stance. Shifting the ball position can influence your swing path and clubface position at impact.

7. **Ensure proper weight transfer**: Golfers who struggle with a slice may not shift their weight adequately to their leading foot during the downswing. Leaving weight on the back foot can cause an open clubface and an outside-in swing path. Focus on correctly transferring weight to encourage a more inside-out swing path and reduce the chances of slicing the ball.

8. **Control body rotation**: Incorporate more rotation of your hips and torso through the swing. An outside-in swing can be caused by a lack of hip movement. Focus on rotating the body more effectively through the ball to promote a better swing path and reduce the tendency to slice.

9. **Practice with different clubs**: Experiment with different clubs to identify if a specific club is causing your slice or push tendencies. Sometimes certain clubs or their specifications may contribute to shot shape issues.

10. **Seek professional instruction**: Consider working with a golf instructor or coach who can analyze your swing, provide personalized guidance, and prescribe specific drills or exercises to correct slices, fades, or pushes.

THE HOOK, THE DRAW, & THE PULL

In golf, a hook, a draw, and a pull are essentially the opposite of the slice, fade, and push, and describe different types of ball flights with a leftward trajectory for a right-handed golfer (or rightward for left-handed golfers). They are also primarily influenced by the clubface alignment and swing path at the point of contact.

Here's a brief explanation of each:

Hook: A shot that curves dramatically from right to left for right-handed players (or vice versa for left-handed players). This is typically unintentional and the result of a closed clubface at impact, often combined with an inside-out swing path, causing a counterclockwise spin on the ball.

The ball starts relatively straight, then veers off to the left of the intended target (or right for left-handed golfers).

Draw: A shot where the golf ball curves gently from right to left for a right-handed player (or vice versa for left-handed players). This typically results from a slightly inside-out swing path with the clubface slightly closed relative to the path, but not as much as a hook.

A draw is a deliberate shot often used by golfers to add distance, to work the ball around obstacles, or on holes where you want your ball to follow the fairway's curves.

Pull: A shot that travels relatively straight but ends up left of the target for right-handed players (or vice versa for left-handed players). It results from an outside-to-inside swing path, where the clubface is square to the swing path but closed to the target line at impact.

While a slice is more common among most golfers, a hook is equally frustrating. Here are Professor MarcO's Top 10 Tips to fix a hook:

1. **Control clubface angle**: Pay attention to your clubface at impact. If it's consistently closed, try to square it up to the target through impact. Practice with alignment aids or seek professional guidance to improve clubface control.

2. **Focus on swing path**: Work on swinging along an inside-out path (for right-handed golfers) or outside-in path (for left-handed golfers) to encourage straighter shots. A swing path that matches your desired shot shape can help fix hooks, draws, or pulls.

3. **Check your grip**: If you're hitting a hook, try to use a weaker grip. Check to make sure your grip isn't too strong, where the hands are turned too much to the right (for right-handed golfers). Adjust your hand position to a more neutral grip by turning your hands slightly to the left.

4. **Manage your grip pressure**: We're typically told to grip lightly, but if you hook the ball, gripping the club a little tighter can help, particularly with more pressure on your left hand. Avoid gripping the club too tightly to promote a smooth release of the club.

5. **Monitor your alignment**: Make sure your body and clubface are aligned properly with the target. Practice setting up square to the target to promote more accurate shots.

6. **Adjust ball position**: Experiment with moving the ball slightly forward in your stance to help reduce hooks or pulls. Shifting the ball position can influence your swing path and clubface position at impact.

7. **Ensure proper weight transfer**: Golfers who tend to hook the ball might be shifting their weight too aggressively or prematurely to the leading foot. This can result in an inside-out swing path and a closed clubface at impact. Work on more balanced and timed weight transfer during your swings to prevent a hook.

8. **Control body rotation**: Rotating your body too aggressively during the downswing can lead to an inside-out swing path and a prematurely closed clubface. An overly active upper body allowing the arms to rotate too soon can cause your hands to flip, also resulting in a closed clubface. You may need to slow down your body rotation to maintain a more square clubface at impact.

9. **Practice with different clubs**: Experiment with different clubs to identify if a specific club is causing your hook or pull tendencies. Sometimes certain clubs or their specifications may contribute to shot shape issues.

10. **Seek professional instruction**: Consider working with a golf instructor or coach who can analyze your swing, provide personalized guidance, and prescribe specific drills or exercises to correct hooks, draws, or pulls.

Both a hook and a slice can be corrected by working on the fundamental aspects of your swing mechanics, such as grip, swing path, and clubface control. Fixing shot shape issues takes time and practice, so be patient. It is also beneficial to seek guidance from a qualified instructor who can provide personalized feedback and drills to help you correct these shot patterns. Consistency and repetition are key to improving your ball flight and accuracy.

PRACTICING

Golf demands precision, timing, and technique, all of which can only be honed through repetition. Consistent practice helps to develop muscle memory, allowing golfers to execute swings and shots more effortlessly and accurately. Only with practice and experience can golfers improve their adaptability to varying course conditions and situations and learn to understand and control ball flight, distance, and direction.

Note from the Professor:

> *Remember, practice makes perfect! It is astounding to me how many golfers expect to get better, but rarely if ever practice!*
>
> *Professional golfers hit THOUSANDS OF BALLS each month if not each week.*

Here are Professor MarcO's Top 20 Tips for practicing your golf game:

1. **Establish a routine**: Develop a consistent practice routine that includes warm-up, drills, simulated game situations, and cool-down exercises.

2. **Set clear goals**: Define specific goals for each practice session, such as improving your putting or working on your driving accuracy.

3. **Warm up**: Begin with a warm-up routine that includes stretches and exercises to loosen up your muscles and prepare your body for practice.

4. **Practice with a purpose**: Focus on specific aspects of your game during practice, such as alignment, tempo, or swing mechanics.

5. **Focus on quality over quantity**: Practice with intent and focus on quality repetitions rather than mindlessly hitting a large number of balls. Ensure each shot has a purpose, and each practice session has a focus.

6. **Incorporate drills**: Integrate various practice drills into your routine to focus on specific skills and reinforce proper mechanics.

7. **Practice time management**: Allocate dedicated time for each aspect of your game, such as driving, iron play, short game, and putting, to ensure well-rounded practice.

8. **Start small**: Begin your practice session with short game drills, such as chipping and putting, to work on your feel and touch around the greens.

9. **Visualize shots**: Before hitting each shot, visualize the intended trajectory, target, and landing area. This helps enhance your mental game and shot execution.

10. **Target variety**: Use different targets or create target areas during practice to simulate on-course scenarios and enhance your precision.

11. **Work on your weaknesses**: Don't just practice the shots you're good at. Identify your weaknesses and spend extra time practicing those areas to improve and gain confidence in those aspects of your game.

12. **Mix up practice clubs**: Vary the clubs you use during practice to develop versatility and adaptability. Practice with different irons, hybrids, and woods.

13. **Practice short game ratio**: Allocate a significant portion of your practice time to the short game, as it can have a substantial impact on your overall score.

14. **Practice short putts**: Improving your putting can significantly lower your scores. Focus on distance control and maintaining a consistent stroke. Practice different lengths and breaks.

15. **Practice course management**: Simulate on-course scenarios during practice, considering different lies, slopes, and club selections to enhance your decision-making skills.

16. **Practice in different conditions**: Practice different lies, terrains, courses, and weather conditions, such as wind or rain, to develop adaptability and learn how different conditions affect your shots.

17. **Simulate pressure**: Create pressure situations during practice, such as setting score goals or playing competitive games with practice partners, to improve your ability to perform under pressure.

18. **Stay positive and patient**: Golf is as much a mental game as a physical one. Maintain a positive mindset during practice and be patient with yourself. Improvement takes time. Practice visualization, focus, and staying calm under pressure.

19. **Track progress**: Keep track of your practice sessions and monitor your progress over time. Note areas of improvement and areas that still need work.

20. **Record and review**: Use video recording tools to capture your swing and review it to identify areas for improvement. Seek feedback from a coach if possible.

Note from the Professor:

> *I must emphasize—watch yourself on video! Given the accessibility of video technology and the growing emphasis on swing analysis and improvement, any golfer who has never used video or seen themselves hit a golf ball on video needs to try out this technology ASAP.*
>
> *Combined with feedback from a coach, it will do wonders for your swing. Many golfers, both amateur and professional, utilize video analysis as a valuable tool for understanding their swing mechanics, identifying areas for improvement, and making adjustments to enhance their performance.*

Effective practice involves deliberate focus, repetition, and an emphasis on specific areas of your game. By following these practice tips, you can maximize your practice sessions and make significant strides in improving your golf skills.

PRE-SHOT ROUTINE

A pre-shot routine can help you focus, eliminate distractions, and prepare yourself mentally and physically for each shot. Customize your routine based on what works best for you and practice it diligently to build confidence and consistency in your game.

Here are Professor MarcO's Top 20 Tips to incorporate into your pre-shot routine:

1. **Consistency**: Develop a consistent pre-shot routine that you can replicate on every shot. This helps create a sense of familiarity and confidence.

2. **Establish a routine timing**: Develop a consistent timing pattern for your routine. This helps create rhythm and a sense of timing in your swing.

3. **Visualize the shot**: Visualize the intended shot and its trajectory before stepping up to the ball. Imagine the desired ball flight and where it will land.

4. **Select your club**: Select the appropriate club based on the shot you want to hit and the distance to the target. Consider factors such as wind, hazards, and elevation changes.

5. **Visualize the target line**: Stand behind the ball and visualize the target line from a face-on perspective. Picture a line extending from the target through the ball.

6. **Check alignment**: Align your feet, hips, and shoulders parallel to the target line. Use an intermediate target to help with alignment.

7. **Breathe**: Take a deep breath to relax and focus your mind. Clear any distractions and be present in the moment.

8. **Relax your grip**: Maintain a relaxed grip pressure on the club. A firm grip can lead to tension and restricted movement in the swing.

9. **Practice swings**: Take a few practice swings to groove the desired swing motion and feel the tempo and rhythm of the swing.

10. **Positive self-talk**: Use positive affirmations or self-talk to reinforce confidence and belief in your abilities. Encourage yourself with positive thoughts.

11. **Quiet the mind**: Quiet your mind and focus on the task at hand. Let go of any previous shots or distractions and be fully present for the current shot.

12. **Narrow focus**: Narrow your focus to a specific target or spot where you want the ball to land. This helps direct your attention and concentration.

13. **Target confirmation**: Reconfirm the target and the desired shot shape in your mind. Picture the ball flying toward the target.

14. **Final alignment check**: Step up to the ball and recheck your alignment. Ensure your body and clubface are aligned correctly to the target.

15. **Waggle**: Take a waggle or a rehearsal swing to loosen up and get a feel for the swing rhythm before addressing the ball.

16. **Check ball position**: Ensure the position of the ball is appropriate for the club and the shot you are going to make.

17. **Check clubface alignment**: Check that the clubface is square to the target. Use alignment aids or markings on the clubface for reference.

18. **Visualize impact**: Imagine the moment of impact and visualize a clean, solid strike. Picture the ball starting on the intended line.

19. **Trust your swing**: Have confidence in your swing and trust the work you've put into practice. Let go of doubt and trust your abilities.

20. **Commit fully**: Once you've completed your routine, commit fully to the shot. Trust your decisions and commit to executing the shot with confidence.

A pre-shot routine is a key factor in achieving both consistency and success in the game of golf. By establishing a pre-shot routine, you'll be able to reproduce successful shots more easily, even under pressure.

COURSE MANAGEMENT

Golf course management is the strategic approach a player uses to navigate the golf course in the fewest number of strokes possible. These decisions must take into account a golfer's abilities, course layout, hole location, wind and weather conditions, hazards, and risk-reward trade-offs.

Here are Professor MarcO's Top 20 Tips for effective course management:

1. **Know your game**: Play according to your skill level, not the skill level you aspire to be. Understand your strengths, weaknesses, and tendencies to make decisions on the course.

2. **Play to your strengths**: Capitalize on your strengths by playing shots that suit your natural shot shape and abilities.

3. **Weigh risk and reward**: Evaluate the risk and reward of each shot, and consider alternatives when risk is high. Avoid taking unnecessary risks and play shots that you can confidently execute.

4. **Play it safe**: Avoid taking unnecessary risks and play shots that you can confidently execute. Sometimes the best strategy is to lay up instead of attempting a more challenging shot.

5. **Prioritize accuracy**: Accuracy is often more important than distance. Focus on hitting fairways and greens, and avoiding trouble spots.

6. **Assess the situation**: Evaluate the course conditions, weather, hazards, and yardages to make smart decisions.

7. **Choose the right tee box**: Play from a tee box that matches your skill level and distance capabilities.

8. **Play smart off the tee**: Use conservative club choices or layups to position yourself in the fairway and set up easier approach shots.

9. **Plan your shots**: Visualize each shot before executing it, considering the best landing areas and shot trajectories. Start from the green and work your way backward, considering the best approach for each hole.

10. **Take note of pin positions**: Be aware of pin positions on each green to strategically plan your approach shots and avoid difficult putts.

11. **Avoid trouble**: Minimize risks by avoiding hazards, trouble spots, and tight areas where your accuracy might be compromised. Try to leave your ball in areas where you're confident in your next shot.

12. **Consider your scoring opportunities**: Identify holes where you have a good chance of making birdie or par and focus on capitalizing on those opportunities.

13. **Manage Par 5s**: Strategize your approach to par 5s, considering layups, risk-reward opportunities, and green accessibility.

14. **Use course knowledge**: Familiarize yourself with the course layout, including doglegs, elevation changes, and prevailing winds.

15. **Adapt to course conditions**: Adjust your strategy based on course conditions, such as firm or soft fairways, fast or slow greens, etc.

16. **Study the greens**: Accurately reading the green can result in fewer putts per round, saving you strokes and improving your score.

17. **Factor in wind and weather**: Adjust your club selection and shot strategy based on wind direction, speed, and weather conditions.

18. **Maintain good pace of play**: Playing too slowly can disrupt your rhythm, and playing too fast can lead to rushed shots.

19. **Stay mentally composed**: Don't let the previous shots affect your current one. Avoid the temptation to recover lost strokes all at once. Maintain focus, manage emotions, and avoid rushing your shots, especially in pressure situations.

20. **Stay positive and flexible**: Adapt to changing circumstances, embrace challenges, and maintain a positive mindset throughout the round.

Effective course management requires a blend of strategic thinking, self-awareness, and adaptability. By implementing these pieces of advice, you can optimize your approach to each hole and improve your overall scoring potential.

IMPROVING CONSISTENCY

"THE ONLY THING CONSISTENT ABOUT MY
GOLF GAME IS MY INCONSISTENCY."

Here are Professor MarcO's Top 20 Tips to become more consistent in golf:

1. **Develop a repeatable swing**: Work on creating a consistent and repeatable swing that feels comfortable to you.

2. **Focus on tempo and rhythm**: Develop a smooth and balanced swing tempo that promotes consistency and reduces unnecessary tension. Avoid a rushed transition from the backswing to the downswing.

3. **Don't overswing**: Focus on solid contact and compressing the ball rather than swinging hard.

4. **Focus on fundamentals**: Pay attention to the basics, ensuring you have the correct grip, posture, alignment, and ball position every time. Consistency starts with a solid foundation.

5. **Establish a pre-shot routine**: Develop a consistent pre-shot routine that helps you focus and prepare for each shot.

6. **Aim correctly**: Make sure you are always aiming at your target before swinging

7. **Play your natural shot shape**: Understand your own swing and play to your strengths. Trying to fight against your natural tendencies can lead to inconsistency.

8. **Play within your abilities**: Understand your skill level and play shots that you can comfortably execute. Play conservatively and don't get overly aggressive.

9. **Improve course management**: Learn to assess risk and reward, making strategic choices that minimize mistakes and optimize scoring opportunities. Take smart risks, not unnecessary ones.

10. **Work on your short game**: Dedicate time to improving your chipping, pitching, and putting. Consistency around the green can save you many strokes.

11. **Know your distances**: Knowing how far you hit each club in your bag can lead to more predictable results.

12. **Play with properly fitted equipment**: Ensure your clubs are fitted to your swing characteristics, helping you consistently strike the ball.

13. **Manage expectations**: Understand that golf is a game of patience and accept that not every shot will be perfect. Stay composed and move on from mistakes.

14. **Control your emotions**: Don't let one bad shot affect the next one. Maintain a positive and focused mindset throughout the round, regardless of previous shots or outcomes.

15. **Analyze and learn from mistakes**: Assess your rounds objectively and identify patterns or areas for improvement to learn and grow from each experience.

16. **Build mental resilience**: Learn to handle pressure and setbacks with resilience, maintaining focus and confidence during challenging situations.

17. **Maintain physical fitness**: Strength and flexibility can help improve the consistency of your swing. Maintain a level of fitness that supports good posture, flexibility, and endurance throughout the round.

18. **Develop a positive routine for practice**: Structure your practice sessions with specific goals and drills to target areas that need improvement.

19. **Invest in lessons**: Work with a qualified golf instructor who can identify areas for improvement and provide personalized guidance to correct flaws in your technique.

20. **Practice regularly**: Dedicate regular practice time to hone your skills and reinforce muscle memory. The more you practice, the more consistent your game will become.

Consistency in golf takes time and effort, and is a product of practice and understanding your own game. Implement these pieces of advice into your golf routine and remain dedicated to improving your skills. Remember, consistency is a journey, and with practice, patience, and a positive mindset, you can gradually become a more consistent golfer.

GOLF TRAINING AIDS

When it comes to learning aids in golf, there are various tools and aids available to help golfers improve their skills. If you're looking for some training aids, it's important to first ask yourself what you want to improve about your game. Once you know what you want to achieve, you can choose aids that will help you reach your goals.

Here are Professor MarcO's Top 20 Tips for golf learning and training aids:

1. **Alignment Sticks**: Lightweight rods used to improve shot alignment and accuracy during practice and on the course.

2. **Putting Alignment Mirror**: A mirror that helps golfers align their eyes, shoulders, and putter face for better putting setup and more accurate putting.

3. **Putting Mat**: A portable, indoor mat that simulates green conditions. It's often marked with lines for alignment and distance control, helping to improve putting accuracy and consistency.

4. **Putting Arc**: Devices that guide your putting stroke along a specific arc or path to assist in developing a consistent putting stroke.

5. **Putt Training Lasers**: A laser device that attaches to your putter and aids in visualizing and aligning putts.

6. **Pressure Putt Trainers**: A portable device designed with a parabolic curve to simulate the pressure of making putts, giving great feedback for getting the pace just right. It is excellent for improving putting skills and accuracy under pressure.

7. **Swing Trainer**: A variety of devices designed to help golfers improve and understand their swing mechanics and develop a more consistent swing.

8. **Swing Weight Trainer**: A specialized club designed with extra weight. It helps to build swing strength, increase clubhead speed, and stretch muscles used during the swing.

9. **Golf Training Mat**: A portable practice mat that allows you to simulate hitting shots from different lies and surfaces.

10. **Golf Nets**: Allow for practicing full swings in limited space, such as your backyard or garage. They are designed to safely contain balls hit with irons, hybrids, and woods, and are typically used with a hitting mat to simulate the feel of a fairway or tee box.

11. **Swing Speed Radar**: This device measures swing speed using radar technology, helping golfers monitor and understand their swing speed, which can lead to better control and longer drives.

12. **Golf Swing Analyzer**: A digital tool that can track and analyze your swing. It often uses sensors or video analysis to provide feedback on various swing metrics including swing speed, club path, and other key metrics.

13. **Swing Plane Trainer**: These devices help golfers maintain the correct swing plane throughout the swing.

14. **Grip Trainer**: A simple but effective tool for learning and reinforcing the correct grip for more control and consistency.

15. **Golf Swing Tempo Trainer**: These aids help golfers establish a consistent and smooth swing tempo.

16. **Wrist and Arm Band**: A band that attaches to the golfer's lead arm and wrist to help maintain proper wrist and arm positions during the swing, preventing excessive wrist bending (cupping or bowing) during the swing.

17. **Posture Correction Belt**: Designed to promote better body and spinal alignment during the golf swing.

18. **Chipping Net**: A portable net that allows you to practice short game shots and improve accuracy around the greens. It often includes targets for improving accuracy.

19. **Impact Bag**: A durable bag designed to absorb the impact of golf swings. It allows golfers to practice and improve their impact position and ball striking.

20. **Impact Tape**: A strip of tape applied to the clubface to provide visual feedback on contact and clubface alignment.

And here are a few extra, because we could all use as much help as we can get!

21. **Launch Monitor**: Measures detailed data on your ball flight, including distance, trajectory, and spin.

22. **Video and Video Swing Analysis Software**: Record and analyze your golf swing using video footage. The software allows you to slow down, pause, and replay your swing, often with additional tools to analyze and review your swing and find areas for improvement.

23. **Golf Simulator**: Provides a realistic and immersive indoor golfing experience by simulating famous courses and providing detailed swing analysis and shot data.

24. **Golf GPS Rangefinders**: Assist in accurate distance measurement to the hole or specific targets, helping golfers select the right club.

25. **Golf Books and Instructional Videos**: Educational resources provide valuable insights and instruction from golf experts.

There are many different learning and training aids available, so it is important to experiment with a variety of them to find the ones that work best for you. They can complement your practice and training routine, helping you develop specific aspects of your game. It's important to use them in conjunction with proper instruction and feedback to maximize their effectiveness and improve your performance on the golf course.

"I CAN'T TELL MY WIFE MY HANDICAP IS GETTING LOWER. SHE'LL WANT TO KNOW WHY I'M NOT HOME ANY EARLIER."

CONCLUSION

You've made it to the end! I can't guarantee that you'll become an expert overnight, but as you close this book I hope you're well on your way to becoming a better golfer.

You may have picked up on a common theme. Practice is key, particularly practice with intention and purpose. The best way to improve your golf skills is to identify your problem areas and practice, practice, practice.

We've addressed crucial aspects of your golf game like mastering swing mechanics, perfecting your short game, and honing mental focus. I encourage you to put these lessons into practice. You've now got the tools in your golf bag to navigate the course with confidence, avoiding the hooks and slices that can veer you off course.

As you set this book down and pick up your clubs, remember that each swing, each round, and each moment on the green is an opportunity for improvement, learning, and enjoyment. The path to becoming a great golfer isn't a straight drive—it's a winding journey filled with rewarding challenges. Embrace the journey and let the love of the game guide you.

These tips are always a great resource to come back to. In golf, as in life, it's always about the next shot.

Now go out there, and make every swing count!

ABOUT THE AUTHOR

MARC OSTROFSKY is an American entrepreneur, venture capitalist, *New York Times* bestselling author and public speaker.

Ostrofsky created, developed, and sold a number of successful telecommunication, publishing, and Internet-based companies. He was a founder of the domain name resale market, was called a "Technology Wildcatter" by the *Houston Chronicle*, and is known for his sale of the domain name Business.com for $7.5 million which landed in the *Guinness Book of World Records* as the most expensive domain name ever sold at the time. He then invested in Business.com which later sold for $345 million.

He still owns a variety of high quality domains and online businesses. Throughout his career, his websites have done $1 Billion in sales and his businesses have won awards including the Inc. 500 and the Ernst & Young Entrepreneur of the Year Award.

Ostrofsky serves on multiple boards helping entrepreneurs and senior executives build, manage and ultimately sell their companies.

Learn more about Marc Ostrofsky and his latest projects at marcostrofsky.com.

ALSO BY MARC OSTROFSKY

Get Rick Click! The Ultimate Guide to Making Money on the Internet (2011)
Instructions and real-life examples from successful internet entrepreneurs on how to succeed with online business models.

Word of Mouse: 101+ Trends in How We Buy, Sell, Live, Learn, Work, And Play (2013)
Insights for consumers and marketers on how to take advantage of the ever-evolving technologies that shape our daily lives.

1001+ Funny Golf Quotes
Ostrofsky teamed up with golf icon Gary McCord to launch the funniest book of golf quotes ever! *Estimated release in 2024.* Join the waitlist at funnygolfquotes.com/sign-up/

More of **Professor MarcO's Top 20 Tips** are coming soon! These compact and actionable guides harness the power of A.I. tools like ChatGPT to compile the best advice on a variety of topics, from weight loss to investing and more.

Scan the QR Code below to view all titles by *New York Times* bestselling author Marc Ostrofsky.